S0-AWV-668

SCIENTIFIC AMERICAN

Gravity, and How It Works

Earth's Journey Through Space
Electromagnetism, and How It Works
Gravity, and How It Works
Great Extinctions of the Past
Great Inventions of the 20th Century
Great Moments in Space Exploration
Volcanic Eruptions, Earthquakes, and Tsunamis
Weather, and How It Works

Jedicke, Peter.
Gravity, and how it
works
WITHDRAWN
c2008.
33305218707887
bk 03/01/10

SCIENTIFIC AMERICAN

Gravity, and How It Works

By Peter Jedicke

CHELSEA HOUSE PUBLISHERS
An imprint of Infobase Publishing

Scientific American: Gravity and How It Works

Copyright © 2008 by Infobase Publishing

Scientific American is a registered trademark of Scientific American, Inc. Its use is pursuant to a license with Scientific American, Inc.

All rights reserved. No part of this book may be reproduced or utilized in any form or by any means, electronic or mechanical, including photocopying, recording, or by any information storage or retrieval systems, without permission in writing from the publisher. For information contact:

Chelsea House
An imprint of Infobase Publishing
132 West 31st Street
New York NY 10001

Library of Congress Cataloging-in-Publication Data

Jedicke, Peter.
Gravity, and how it works / Peter Jedicke.
p. cm. — (Scientific american)
Includes bibliographical references and index.
ISBN-13: 978-0-7910-9051-0 (hardcover)
ISBN-10: 0-7910-9051-5 (hardcover)
1. Gravity—Juvenile literature. I. Title. II. Series.
QC178.J43 2007
531′.14—dc22 2007017785

Chelsea House books are available at special discounts when purchased in bulk quantities for businesses, associations, institutions, or sales promotions. Please call our Special Sales Department in New York at (212) 967-8800 or (800) 322-8755.

You can find Chelsea House books on the World Wide Web at http://www.chelseahouse.com

Series design by Gilda Hannah
Cover design by Takeshi Takahashi and Joo Young An

Printed in the United States of America

Bang GH 10 9 8 7 6 5 4 3 2 1

This book is printed on acid-free paper.

All links and Web addresses were checked and verified to be correct at the time of publication. Because of the dynamic nature of the Web, some addresses and links may have changed since publication and may no longer be valid.

Contents

CHAPTER ONE
Downward Motion 7

CHAPTER TWO
The Clockwork Universe 15

CHAPTER THREE
Universal Gravity 24

CHAPTER FOUR
The Triumph of Gravity 32

CHAPTER FIVE
Einstein's Universe 41

CHAPTER SIX
Dark Matter 49

Glossary 58
Bibliography 59
Further Exploration 61
Index 62
About the Author 64
Picture Credits 64

CHAPTER ONE

Downward Motion

A grapefruit is nice and round, and just heavy enough that it will make a good, strong thump on the ground when it is dropped. Yet, it would make a big splat if it fell from the balcony of a tall building. Why does it break open only when it is dropped from a greater height, and not when simply released from your hand to the floor? The obvious answer might be that the grapefruit hits the ground harder when it falls a longer distance. But how does the grapefruit know how far it is falling, or how hard it should hit the ground?

If you decide to study this kind of question by coming up with a possible answer and then testing it to see if it's true, that's called science. These tests are called **experiments**. You might suggest that a grapefruit has a rocket motor inside, but it wouldn't take long to think up a way to test that—just cut it open and you'll see that it's just juice and pulp. Maybe you would then suggest that some sort of power outside of the grapefruit makes it hit the ground harder when dropped from a greater height. This **theory** is a more reasonable suggestion, of course. Theories are tested again and again in a variety of situations to try to prove that they are correct. If what happens in each test always matches what a theory predicted would happen, then the theory is a good one.

Nevertheless, scientists can never be absolutely, totally certain that a theory will always pass whatever test comes next. Eventually, after many tests and perhaps some updates to their ideas, scientists gain confidence in their theory and call it a scientific law. The scientific law that explains what happens to a grapefruit when it falls—or to a rock or a raindrop when they fall—is the law of **gravity**.

The Science Behind a Grapefruit

The experiments that lead to a theory—and then perhaps to a scientific law—usually involve measurements. This means that scientists must come up with numbers that describe some part of what happens when a grapefruit falls. Using numbers is important in science because number descriptions can be compared

GREEK SCIENCE

In ancient Greece 2,500 years ago, the most educated people were the philosophers. In those days, lectures and reading were the only ways to learn. There were no laboratories or scientific experiments. Although the Greek thinkers were wrong about a lot of things, they wanted to come up with explanations that made sense, instead of just believing in magic and myth. Philosophers like Socrates, Plato, and Aristotle tried to understand the world by discussing what they thought was sensible.

Aristotle wrote that real things were made of the four elements called earth, fire, air, and water. Each of the four elements had a natural place, and Aristotle believed that motion occurred because objects would move toward those natural places. He said that the natural place for any solid object was at the center of the Earth. Once an object was as close to the center of the Earth as possible, it would stop moving, all on its own. According to Aristotle, the Sun, Moon, planets, and stars obeyed different rules since they did not belong to the human world. If a person was happy with this explanation, there was no need to explore other theories such as gravity. Therefore, for centuries no one bothered to create better explanations for how the world works.

much more carefully than word descriptions, which depend on someone's opinion or how someone feels about what happened.

For a falling grapefruit, two obvious things that a scientist would want to measure would be the distance that the grapefruit falls and the time it takes to fall. Distance is measured along a line—either a straight line in simple situations or sometimes along complicated, curving paths. It is important to note that every measurement requires a unit to express the measurement so that other people will know what the measurement means. It makes no sense to say that a grapefruit falls "61," because everyone would ask "61 what?" In the United States, the system that is the most widely used involves inches and feet and many other units, but scientists around the world use units called the International System. This is also known as the metric system. In this book, the U.S. measurement will be given first, followed by the equivalent metric measurement; whenever calculations are performed, however, the metric measures will be used.

There's something interesting about the distance a grapefruit falls and the time that it takes to fall. How far the grapefruit falls is up to you; it's your grapefruit. You decide where to drop it, and when. Then, after you let it go, the grapefruit seems to be on its own. But is it really? Good scientists repeat their experiments, and if you drop a grapefruit many times from a height of 100 feet (30.5 meters), it always takes about 2.5 seconds to hit the ground. That is because the grapefruit's speed is not really up to the grapefruit itself. The pattern of distance versus speed shows that nature has a rule to determine how quickly the grapefruit falls. Further experiments demonstrate that the same is true for any other thing, so long as the object doesn't float in the air like a leaf or a paper airplane. In fact, the law of gravity doesn't tell one object apart from another. All objects fall in the same way; if you drop an apple from a certain height several times, that apple will always take about the same amount of time to hit the ground. The behavior of a falling object is not determined by anything about the object itself, but rather by gravity.

What about a different height? If the grapefruit falls from 200 feet (61 m), would it take twice as long to fall? What about 300 feet (91 m), or more? If you could do this experiment over and over from different heights, here is what you would learn:

Downward Distance Versus Time Required

Feet	Meters	Seconds
100	30.5	2.5
200	61	3.5
400	122	5.0
800	244	7.0
1200	366	8.6
1600	488	10
3200	975	14
4800	1460	17.2

Compare the time it takes the grapefruit to fall from 400 feet (122 m) with the time from 100 feet (30.5 m), and then from 800 feet (244 m), and 200 feet (61 m), and so on. You will notice that the grapefruit takes twice as long to fall from four times the height. It appears that the grapefruit is not only falling rapidly, but also actually speeding up as it falls. A change in speed is called an **acceleration**. Scientists measure acceleration by dividing a measured change in speed by the time it takes the speed to change. And it turns out that every object, everywhere around the world, no matter how heavy or large it is, changes its speed in the same way as it falls. (That is, provided it doesn't flutter or coast in the air.) The acceleration for everything is roughly the same: an increase of 32 feet per second every second (or 9.8 meters per second every second).

Galileo's Experiments with Ramps

It's not so easy to measure time accurately over only a few seconds. Before there were electronic stopwatches or even accurate

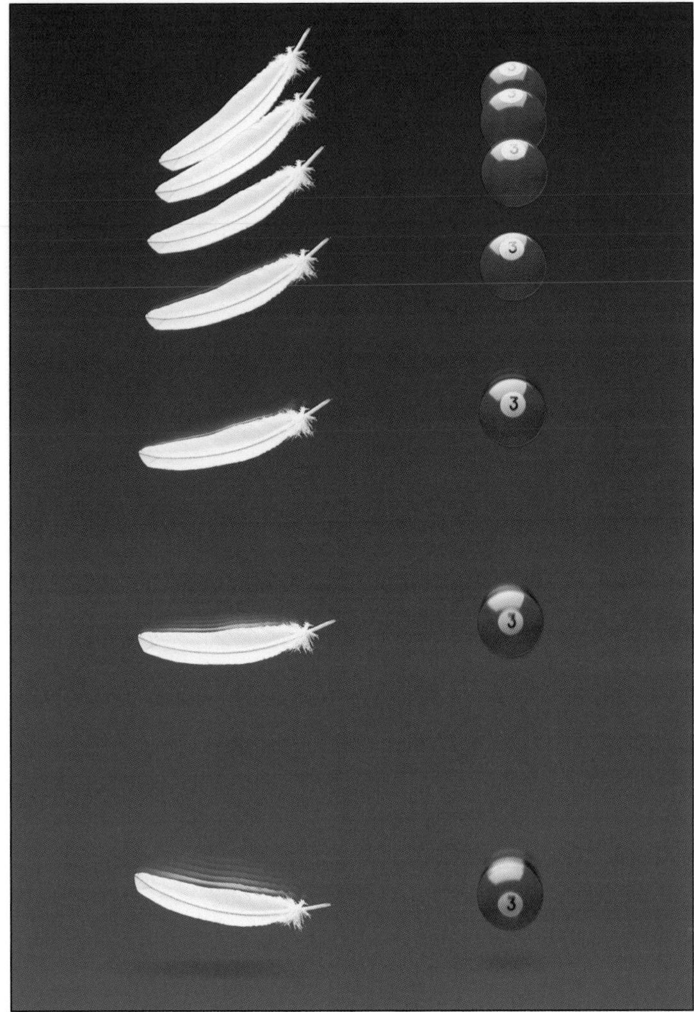

When dropped from the same height, a feather and a heavy billiard ball fall to the ground at the same constant rate. This phenomenon is due to gravity.

clocks at all, a European scientist named Galileo Galilei (1564–1642) was the first person to succeed at carefully measuring the time it takes a falling object to get to the ground.

Galileo was well known in his time for coming up with clever experiments and explaining them very clearly. To ease the problem of measuring the swift downward motion of an object, Galileo built ramps made of wood. The ramps were long enough to reach across a typical school classroom. He carefully cut a smooth, straight groove in the ramp, lifted one end a bit, and rolled a polished bronze ball down it. The idea was that the

Italian scientist Galileo Galilei was the first person to calculate an object's rate of acceleration when falling. After performing many experiments, he determined a mathematical law for acceleration, which proved that objects of various weights increase in speed at a constant rate as they fall to the ground.

motion of the ball always proceeded in a similar way, whether it fell from a height or rolled down a ramp.

To measure time, Galileo used a jug of water that had a narrow pipe near the bottom. He hung the jug so that the small jet of water from the pipe was collected in a glass. Very carefully, he would open the pipe just as he released the bronze ball at the top of the ramp, and close it again when the ball got to the bottom. Then he would set the glass of water aside and compare it with the glass of water collected in the next run of his experiment. Galileo did this hundreds of times, with the bronze ball rolling various distances and the ramp set to various slopes. He then organized the results into a table and looked for the pattern in the numbers. Even though the bronze ball rolled much more slowly than a grapefruit would fall when dropped straight downward, the rule was the same: the ball took twice as long to roll four times as far. In this way, Galileo became the first scientist to measure acceleration caused by gravity.

GALILEO AND THE TOWER OF PISA

One of the most appealing legends in the history of science concerns Galileo and the famed Tower of Pisa. According to the story, Galileo climbed to the top of the tower and dropped two balls at the same time. One was a very heavy cannonball and the other was much lighter, perhaps made of wood or simply a smaller ball of iron. According to Aristotle's theory, a heavier object would have a greater need to get to its natural place—as close to the center of Earth as possible. That seemed to make sense back then, because it is certainly harder to hold up a heavy object than it is to hold up a light one. Doesn't that mean that a heavy object is trying harder to get closer to the center of Earth? If Aristotle were right, the cannonball should fall to the ground much more quickly than the lighter object. But this isn't the case, and Galileo knew it: if two balls are dropped together, they hit the ground together, regardless of how much each one weighs.

Although Galileo wrote books about his observations—and the books made him very famous—he never wrote about an experiment at the Tower of Pisa. Later, when Galileo was an old man, a journalist interviewed him about his life as a scientist. It was probably the journalist who made up the story of the Tower of Pisa.

The leaning Tower of Pisa is the bell tower of the Duomo, a medieval cathedral, in the city of Pisa in Tuscany, Italy. The tower's slant is especially obvious when it is viewed next to the cathedral.

Along with figuring out how fast gravity would make an object fall, Galileo used his observations with the ramp to come to another important conclusion. He wondered whether an object moved on its own or whether an outside influence was required to move it. It's a confusing question because, on the one hand, living things like humans seem to have total control of our own motion; but on the other hand, non-living objects like a bronze ball need something beyond themselves to move. Galileo's theory was simple, with a twist: he wrote that a non-living object can never change its motion by itself, but that it tends to keep doing whatever it's already doing. So a grapefruit will remain at rest in your hand because you are holding it up against gravity, not because being at rest is somehow special. When you drop it, the grapefruit falls because of gravity's influence, not because the grapefruit itself needs to move downward on its own. With four centuries of experience after Galileo, scientists today are convinced that in experiments involving motion, all objects tend to keep doing what they are already doing. This is called **inertia**.

Another question might be: Why is there gravity at all? But at least until now, no one has ever come up with a reasonable suggestion for an answer to this question. For now, scientists and others practice describing gravity, measuring it, and using it every day. An explanation for why gravity exists will have to wait for a clever person to come up with a good theory.

CHAPTER TWO

The Clockwork Universe

Thousands of years ago in the time of the ancient Babylonians, the major planets could be seen in the night sky just as they can be seen today. Mercury, Venus, Mars, Jupiter, and Saturn have traveled around the solar system thousands of times since those days. From Earth, they appear to rise in the east or set in the west, and their motion can be tracked from day to day against the background stars. This is what astronomers did back then—tracked the planets and stars, year after year, century after century. They kept their records on clay tables in a kind of writing known as cuneiform.

In the fourth century B.C., Babylonian astronomers such as Kidinnu calculated the speed of the Moon's motion around Earth. They even learned how to predict a lunar **eclipse**. They understood that there are fascinating cycles and patterns involved in the world of space.

Claudius Ptolemy was an astronomer who lived in Egypt around the year A.D. 150. Ptolemy analyzed many older texts and scrolls, and also added his own observations of the night sky. What he learned was summarized in a book known today as *The Almagest*. The book includes such marvels as a star catalog, tables

A lunar eclipse occurs when a full moon passes through some portion of Earth's shadow. Although the Moon remains completely within Earth's dark shadow, indirect sunlight still manages to illuminate it.

for predicting eclipses, and descriptions of the motions of the planets. According to Ptolemy, the motions of the major planets, the Sun, and the Moon, could all be explained by perfect spheres nested inside each other, with Earth itself at the center. Outward from Earth, the order of the spheres was the Moon first, then Mercury, Venus, the Sun, Mars, Jupiter, and Saturn. (The ancient astronomers did not know about Uranus and Neptune.) The Sun and the Moon were included because the word *planet* means "wanderer" in the Greek language. The ancient astronomers distinguished the seven "wanderers" from the fixed stars that are now known to be far beyond our own solar system.

Ptolemy most likely did not think of the stars and wanderers as real objects hanging in space and riding on giant spheres. He believed that the shining dots in the night sky were just appearances, and that it wasn't necessary to explain what they really were. Perhaps they were some kind of illusions or even projections of something beyond human understanding. All that mattered was to explain the motions that were observed in the night sky.

But for this explanation, Ptolemy wanted smooth and uniform calculations, whereas observations made it plain to see that the planets do not move in a perfectly uniform way. To describe the variations in their motions, Ptolemy came up with the idea of each wanderer riding on multiple spheres or circles, some larger and some smaller, all connected to each other. Each sphere turned at its own uniform rate, but different from the others. Thus, the uneven appearances of shining dots moving in the sky were the final result of the complicated combination of all the motions of the spheres.

From the modern point of view in astronomy, it is important to note that Ptolemy thought motions in space were completely different from how objects moved on Earth. Gravity was not part

Astronomer Claudius Ptolemy studied the night sky, star paths, and planetary motion, and summarized his observations in what is now known as *The Almagest. The Almagest* is the most important source of information about ancient Greek astronomy.

of Ptolemy's system at all. For centuries, astronomers used Ptolemy's system to predict roughly where the planets would be seen each year.

Putting the Sun at the Center

Meanwhile, other ancient thinkers, such as Aristarchus of Samos, were considering alternative ideas about the planets and stars. Aristarchus suggested a **heliocentric** system: that the Sun is at the center of everything and that Earth and other planets are actual objects that move around the Sun. But the idea that the

THE DAYS OF THE WEEK

There is a fascinating connection between planetary motions and the days of the week. When people name the planets today, they list them in an order that starts with the planet closest to the Sun, and then they move outward from there: Mercury first, then Venus, and so on. But in Ptolemy's time, astronomers didn't apply the concept of distance to the planets at all. They thought Saturn came first, because its motion was explained by a celestial sphere that turned more slowly than all the others. Then came Jupiter, Mars, the Sun, Venus, Mercury, and finally the Moon, closest to Earth.

Educated citizens in those days believed that the planets had a role in everyday life, and that each planet took a turn dominating a single hour of the day, in order. The first hour thus belonged to Saturn, the second to Jupiter, then Mars, the Sun, and so on. The eighth hour was back to Saturn, as was the fifteenth and the twenty-second. Continuing the cycle, the first hour of the second day of the week was the Sun's, the first hour of the third day of the week was the Moon's, and so on. After 168 hours over seven complete days, the cycle would repeat, and that's why we have seven days in a week.

The name of each day of the week came from the planet that dominated the day's first hour. Later cultures adopted this calendar system. The names we use today evolved from Old English names of the Roman mythological gods (for whom the first-discovered planets were named): for example, *Tew's day* (Mars), *Woden's day* (Mercury), *Thor's day* (Jupiter), and *Freya's day* (Venus).

entire Earth could be moving through space seemed ridiculous. The Polish scientist Nicolaus Copernicus brought up the heliocentric theory again in the sixteenth century. Copernicus described the theory in a book that was not published until after his death. Once Copernicus's book was available, European scientists began to debate whether it was possible that Earth was actually moving through space.

Tycho Brahe was an astronomer in Denmark who knew of Copernicus's book and the debate surrounding the heliocentric theory. Brahe was a patient and meticulous scientist and was not satisfied just arguing about the theory. He wanted to get to the bottom of it. He suggested that better measurements were needed in order to compare different descriptions of how the planets moved. Brahe devoted himself to these measurements. The observations he made of the positions of the planets throughout many years were much more precise than any other astronomer's measurements. Brahe's records were then passed on to his student, Johannes Kepler.

What Kepler did with Brahe's observations was astounding. In painstaking detail, he studied the comparisons that Brahe had suggested. Kepler concluded that none of the theories proposed by other scientists were good enough to explain the motions of the planets. Kepler was determined to come up with a new theory that better fit the observations he and Brahe had made.

Kepler's Laws

What Kepler found out was that the paths of the planets and moons are *elliptical*, meaning that they are shaped like ellipses. An **ellipse** is a special kind of oblong circle. It is easy to draw: Put two pins, fairly close together, in a piece of cardboard. Then make a loop of string, put it around the two pins, and use a pencil in the loop to pull it tight. Keeping the string tight, move the pencil around the pins to mark the cardboard. The resulting shape is an ellipse. In this activity, each of the two pins is called a **focus** of the ellipse. Kepler discovered that the Sun is always at

A CASTLE OF THE HEAVENS

Tycho Brahe's father was a Danish nobleman with connections to the King of Denmark. King Frederick II was impressed by Brahe's good reputation and gave him land on a small island called Hveen, not far from the city of Copenhagen. The magnificent observatory that Brahe designed became known as Uraniborg, or "castle to the heavens." Not only was it the most modern astronomical observatory of his time, but also Uraniborg was built complete with gardens and a library, and was home to Brahe, his family, and his staff.

A few years after Uraniborg was built, Brahe had another building constructed nearby, called Stjerneborg, or "castle to the stars." Stjerneborg was devoted solely to astronomical measurements. This was before the invention of the telescope, and so the measuring devices were large metal arcs or circles inscribed with the measurements of angles. One disc was almost 15 feet (5 m) across. These instruments were placed in towers with roofs that could be opened up to the sky. The arcs or circles were either fixed on a wall or mounted on rotating pedestals. Brahe or an assistant would look across one of the discs at a planet in the night sky. They would observe and record the spot on the disc that lined up with the planet. For 20 years, Brahe recorded the positions of planets and stars from Uraniborg and Stjerneborg.

In 1584, Danish astronomer Tycho Brahe built an above and underground observatory called Stjerneborg. Most observations for his star catalogue were made from five chambers that contained instruments under a rotating canopy that provided shelter from the wind, cold, and precipitation.

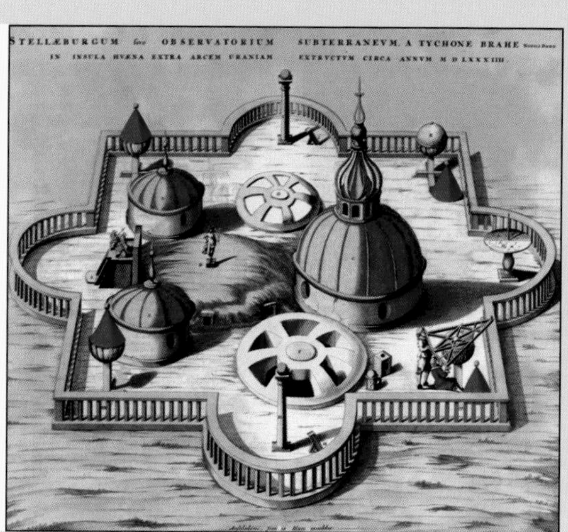

Kepler's first law of planetary motion states that each planet travels in an ellipse with the Sun as its focus. On June 8, 2004 the planet Venus, which appears as a black dot (*above*), was photographed in transit around the Sun.

one focus of every planet's ellipse. Today, we call this Kepler's first law: the path of a planet is an ellipse, with the Sun at one focus.

Kepler also studied the speed of each planet, as calculated from Brahe's records. It's not difficult to work out the average speed of a planet: pick any point in the planet's path and measure how long it takes for the planet to come back to that point. The time it takes is called the **period.** For example, the period of Earth's trip around the Sun is our definition of one year—365 days. A complete revolution, whether in the shape of a circle or an ellipse, is always 360 degrees. Therefore, dividing 360 by the period gives the average speed of the planet.

But at times, the planets travel a bit faster than average, and sometimes they travel slower than average. Even the ancient astronomers recognized this. Kepler looked for a rule to describe this difference in speed. This led to a second remarkable discovery, Kepler's second law. If you draw a line from the Sun to any planet, and follow this line as the planet goes around the Sun,

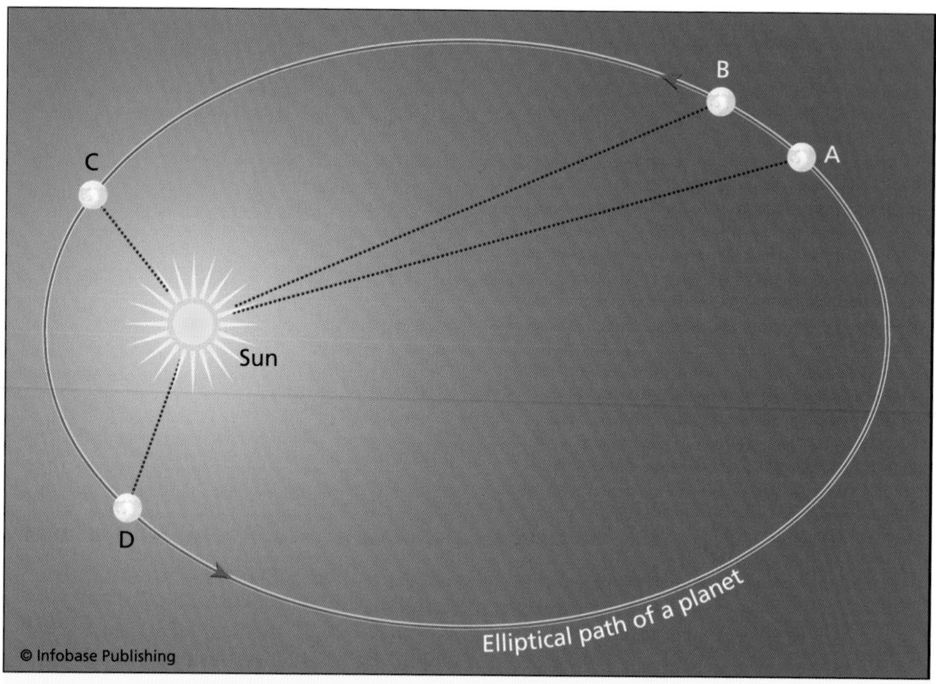

Kepler's second law of planetary motion states that a planet travels faster when it is closer to the Sun. Kepler came to this conclusion when he realized that it takes the same amount of time for a planet to travel from point A to point B as it does to travel from point C to point D.

the line sweeps out a section of the path that looks somewhat like a piece of pie. The planet always moves a little faster when it is a little closer to the Sun, and a little slower when it is far from the Sun. The result is that the pie-shaped section of the path encloses the same area in any equal durations of time. This rule was an important part of Kepler's calculations.

Then there is Kepler's third law. Kepler performed calculations involving the period of each planet known at that time, as well as the average distance of each planet from the Sun. For an ellipse, the average distance is called the semi-major axis, and it is half the distance across the ellipse, through each **focus**, at its greatest width. Kepler **squared** the period, which means multiplying the period by itself. He then cubed the average distance for each planet, which means multiplying the average distance times itself three times. He then divided the one number into the other. He found something quite curious: the answer comes out the same for each of the planets. The following table shows the modern values. Notice that the final column shows almost the same answer for each planet.

PLANETS AND THEIR ORBITS AROUND THE SUN						
Planet	Average Distance from the Sun		Distance Cubed	Period	Period Squared	Ratio
	in millions of miles	in millions of kilometers	in billion billion kilometers squared	in days	in days squared	d^3/T^2
Mercury	36	58	195,000	88	7,700	25.1
Venus	67	108	1,270,000	225	50,600	25.0
Earth	93	150	3,350,000	365	133,000	25.1
Mars	142	228	11,9000,000	687	472.000	25.1
Jupiter	483	778	471,000,000	4,330	18,700,000	25.1
Saturn	887	1,427	2,910,000,000	10,750	116,000,000	25.2
Uranus	1,783	2,869	23,600,000,000	30,660	940,000,000	25.1
Neptune	2,795	4,497	90,900,000,000	60,200	3,620,000,000	25.1

When other astronomers in the seventeenth century read about Kepler's three laws of planetary motion, they were truly amazed. The observations finally made sense. Yet, even Kepler did not discuss how his new laws related to the basic ideas of objects moving and falling under the influence of gravity. It did not occur to him that the same force of gravity that explains everyday objects and movements on Earth could also rule the paths of the planets.

CHAPTER THREE

Universal Gravity

Gravity loves a grapefruit. A grapefruit falls when it is dropped, and when it is thrown upward it eventually comes back down. But can a grapefruit move in two directions at once? On the one hand, the answer seems to be no. An object can't go both up and down, or both left and right, at the same time.

Yet, an object can move in two directions at once: sideways and down. The two motions occur together, but for separate reasons. The grapefruit moves sideways (horizontally) when it is thrown. When the person throwing it lets it go, the grapefruit continues horizontally on its own because of inertia. It would move horizontally forever if it didn't hit the ground. But meanwhile, gravity's influence gradually and steadily draws the grapefruit downward.

That's also what happens when a pitcher throws a baseball. No matter how hard he or she throws the baseball, gravity turns the horizontal path of the ball into a slight downward arc. That's why the pitcher's mound in baseball is permitted to be as much as 10 inches (25.4 cm) above the level of home plate.

In 1687, English scientist and mathematician Sir Isaac Newton published the famed *Philosophiae Naturalis Principia Mathematica*, which stated that gravity applied to all parts of the universe, both Earthly objects and celestial bodies. After studying Kepler's laws of planetary motion, Newton put forth the three universal laws of motion and defined the law of universal gravitation.

The Motion of the Moon

Over very long distances, the arc of a thrown object is important because Earth itself is curved. Imagine a giant slingshot that could throw an object with a horizontal speed faster than any baseball could go. Imagine also that the object never lost speed. As gravity pulled the object downward, it would move so far that the shape of Earth's surface would curve beneath it. While inertia keeps the object moving sideways on its own, gravity pulls it downward until it smacks into the ground. An even faster object, like a modern missile, could go even farther.

In the seventeenth century, Sir Isaac Newton (1642–1727) took this idea to its logical conclusion. He came up with a formula to figure out how fast a person would have to launch a cannonball horizontally from a mountaintop in order to make it go in a complete circle all the way around Earth.

Cannonballs can't really be fired fast enough to do that, but Newton used this example to help illustrate what his formula meant. From a height of about 120 miles (190 kilometers), a horizontal launch speed of 17,400 miles per hour (7,800 meters per second) would take any object around the whole Earth in about 88 minutes without hitting the ground at all. It would be moving sideways at a high speed, and gravity would affect the sideways motion with the exact strength needed for the object's path to match Earth's curve. Gravity tries to pull the object toward the center of Earth, but inertia keeps it going sideways. The path of an object going around any object in space like this is called an **orbit**. This is, in fact, what Kepler called the path in his three laws, and Newton had studied Kepler's work.

Newton's great insight was that gravity reaches everywhere. He knew, for instance, that each of the four large moons of Jupiter travels in its own orbit around the giant planet. All the planets, including Jupiter, orbit the Sun. This means that there must be a tremendously strong force pulling a planet toward the Sun while

NEWTON'S APPLE

In addition to the story of Galileo and the Tower of Pisa, there is a legend about Sir Isaac Newton. As the story goes, Newton suddenly came up with his ideas on gravity after an apple fell off a tree and hit him on the head in the summer of 1666. This is almost certainly not true.

What is true, however, is that Newton wrote about the apple as a useful example of an object under the influence of gravity. Newton suggested that the apple and the Moon were both under the influence of Earth's gravity. Prior to this, scientists had not thought of any strong connection between the motion of spheres in space and everyday motion on Earth. On average, the Moon is about 240,000 miles (384,000 km) away from Earth. When Newton calculated the orbit of an apple around Earth at that distance, he found it would take about 28 days, which is the time the Moon's orbit requires. The Moon must move at 2,300 miles per hour (1,000 m per second) to make it around Earth in that time.

the planet travels through space. In fact, Newton wrote that every object in the universe feels a gravitational pull from every other object in the universe. Today, this idea is called Newton's law of universal gravitation.

In general, any push or pull is called a **force**. There are other kinds of force, but gravity was the first to have a detailed formula to explain it. Because Newton provided a formula, the law of universal gravitation is more than just a vague description of how gravity works. The formula allows a person to calculate the exact strength of the force between any two objects in the universe.

For a larger orbit, the size of the circle or ellipse you draw would get much bigger. Newton realized that this means gravity must spread out through space and must be weaker at greater distances from the Sun or any body in space. Newton also realized that bigger objects have a stronger gravitational force and, since the pull goes both ways, each object must contribute to the force of gravity between them. It is the **mass**—the amount of matter ("stuff") contained in an object—that measures the contribution.

All this is included in Newton's formula, which says: multiply the two masses together, and divide twice by the distance between them. To divide twice (or multiply twice) by a number, a mathematician says you **square** the number, because this is the same arithmetic that is required to figure out the area of a square. When you do all this with the appropriate units, the calculation tells you precisely how strong the gravitational pull between the two objects is. This calculation itself is not really difficult, but an additional multiplication step is required.

This extra multiplication is called the gravitational constant, and Newton explained that it just had to be measured once and then could be applied in every case. After all, Newton's law is universal. To measure the gravitational constant the first time, someone had to perform a very sensitive laboratory experiment involving the force of gravity between objects whose weights were already known, and not including Earth itself. Although Earth's gravity is strong enough to hold you down, the gravitational force between two grapefruits is exceedingly tiny. Because this measurement is such a challenge, it took more than a century after Newton came up with the formula. The scientist who first achieved this was Henry Cavendish. Cavendish used two heavy metal balls, made of lead and weighing about 350 pounds (160 kg) each, mounted about 6 feet (2 meters) apart in a sealed room. A horizontal bar hanging about 39 inches (1 m) from the ceiling, also about 6 feet (2 m) long, and balanced on each end by smaller lead spheres weighing about 1.5 pounds (.7 kg) each, was also part of the equipment. The horizontal bar hung between the two large metal spheres so that the gravity from each of the larger spheres would pull the smaller spheres toward the larger spheres

British scientist Henry Cavendish was the first to accurately calculate the gravitational constant using a torsion balance. A torsion balance is an instrument that measures the gravitational force between two masses, based on the amount they twist a fine wire. Since the gravitational constant was accurately calculated, the mass of the Earth was indirectly calculated as well.

HOW TIDES WORK

Once Newton figured out the law of universal gravitation, he realized that it also explained why Earth's oceans have tides. From one side of Earth to the other is about 7,920 miles (12,700 km)—roughly 3% of the distance from Earth to the Moon. So at any moment, the Moon's gravity is stronger on the side of Earth that is facing the Moon than on the side opposite. The oceans on the side of Earth facing the Moon are actually pulled a small but noticeable distance toward the Moon. Similarly, the oceans on the opposite side of Earth remain a tiny bit farther away. The result is two bulges that slosh around in the oceans on the opposite sides of Earth. These bulges are what we know as tides.

and make the bar twist. The angle of twist was carefully measured by a telescope looking through a hole in the wall.

The strength of the force of gravity between the large spheres and the small spheres was calculated from those measurements, thus establishing the value of the gravitational constant. Today this is called the Cavendish experiment, and it can be performed in many school physics labs.

Gravity at Earth's Surface

The gravitational constant, the mass of Earth, the distance to the center of Earth, and the square of the distance to the center of Earth are all the same in every calculation because these numbers apply to every object on the surface of Earth. That's why part of Newton's formula—the part that has the mass of Earth divided by the distance squared—is the same for every person and object on Earth.

Scientists and students call this amount **g**, and it comes out as an acceleration, that is, as a change in speed divided by the time required. Its value is 32 feet per second-squared (9.8 meters per second-squared). It's because every object shares this part of Newton's formula for the gravitational force from the Earth that all falling objects gain speed in the same way, as Galileo noticed.

HALLEY'S COMET

Newton naturally wanted to receive proper credit for his discoveries. One day his friend Edmund Halley told him that another scientist claimed to have come up with a formula for gravity. Newton told Halley that he himself had worked out all the mathematics years before. Halley encouraged Newton to gather up his notes and write a book. The book was published in 1687 and, although it is long, tedious to read, and written in Latin, it is still famous today as perhaps the most influential book in the history of science.

Halley, an astronomer himself, thought about Newton's rules for orbits and realized that comets must follow the same rules. Yet, although the orbits of the planets and moons are ellipses only slightly different from perfect circles, comet orbits are long and narrow. Halley calculated that one particular comet, previously seen in 1682, would return in 1758. Although Halley did not live to see it again, when the comet did indeed return in 1758, it was named in Halley's honor. The last time Halley's comet was seen from Earth was in 1986. You might see it yourself when it nears Earth again in the year 2061.

British astronomer and mathematician Edmund Halley discovered how to determine the periodic cycles of comets.

Although mass is the measure of the amount of stuff in an object, weight expresses the pull of gravity on that stuff. Usually when someone talks about weight, he or she is referring to the pull of gravity on an object that is on Earth's surface. According to Newton's formula, the force of gravity is weaker if you are farther away. Thus, the weight of an object is less if you take the object far from the surface of Earth. If there were a building tall enough to reach twice as far from the center of Earth as you usually are—about 4,000 miles (6,400 km) above the surface—and you measured the weight of a grapefruit on the roof of the building, it would be reduced to about one-quarter the value you are used to. The grapefruit's weight would be even less if the building were higher still, but it would never be reduced to zero. Of course, climbing up that high would put you well into outer space. Nevertheless, if you dropped the grapefruit, it would fall immediately back to Earth. Remember that putting the grapefruit into orbit would require a very fast sideways speed. Meanwhile, the mass of the grapefruit would be the same wherever you took it—about three-quarters of a pound (.350 kg).

CHAPTER FOUR

The Triumph of Gravity

On October 4, 1957, the former Soviet Union (modern-day Russia) launched Sputnik 1, the first human-made object to orbit Earth. A few months later, a U.S. rocket sent up a rival space satellite called Vanguard 1. Sputnik was as big as a beach ball and weighed as much as an average person, but Vanguard was only the size of a grapefruit. Vanguard was put into a much higher orbit, though, and will still be there in the twenty-second century. Sputnik, on the other hand, was sent into a low orbit; gravity brought it crashing down within 100 days. This was the beginning of the "space race," an intense scientific and technological competition between the United States and the Soviet Union. It lasted through the 1960s and ended in a significant victory for the United States after it landed astronauts on the Moon.

The launch of a rocket is a very exciting thing to see. Riding a thunderous yellow tail of flame, the rocket rises into the blue sky. At first it goes straight up, but soon it turns, and gradually the rocket is moving almost horizontally. Launch engineers usually aim a rocket to the east, and for a very simple reason: the whole Earth is spinning toward the east all the time. Engineers want the

A rocket launches into space from the Kennedy Space Center in Cape Canaveral, Florida. The rocket was launched toward the east in order to keep with Earth's rotation.

rocket to have every possible advantage, and the eastward motion of Earth helps the sideways motion of the rocket. As Sir Isaac Newton explained, the upward thrust is just to get the rocket into space at first. It's the sideways motion of a spacecraft that keeps it in orbit while gravity pulls it toward the center of Earth.

Kinetic Energy and Potential Energy

The motion of a rocket or any other object involves what scientists call **energy**. Simply stated, energy is the ability to make things happen. Motion involves **kinetic energy**, the simplest of the

THE DISCOVERY OF NEPTUNE

Since Sir Isaac Newton's formulas about motion and gravity were published in 1687, scientists have developed many advanced mathematical techniques to apply them to real life. The most dramatic success came almost 70 years after the discovery of the planet Uranus in 1781. Following the discovery, astronomers observed Uranus regularly and carefully recorded its positions in the sky. Although the ellipse of Uranus's orbit was calculated very precisely, there was a problem: the path that astronomers predicted the orbit would take differed from the path it actually took.

Although the difference was small, it was enough to catch the attention of Urbain Jean Joseph Le Verrier (1811–1877), a French expert in astronomical calculations. He decided that the difference between the predicted orbit and the actual orbit could be caused by the gravity of another planet beyond Uranus. Le Verrier then figured out where the undiscovered planet could be seen in the night sky. He contacted the director of the Berlin Observatory with instructions for where to look, and it turned out that a student there had prepared a new star map that just happened to cover the proper area of the sky. Neptune, the eighth planet, was discovered on the first night the Berlin astronomers looked for it—September 23, 1846.

The planet Neptune, as seen by the spacecraft Voyager 2, was first discovered on September 23, 1846 based on a mathematical prediction. French mathematician Urbain Jean Joseph Le Verrier correctly theorized that a then-unobserved planet was disturbing Uranus's orbit.

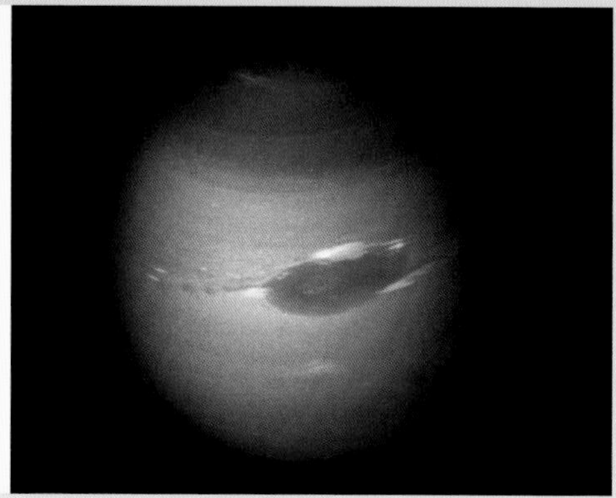

many forms of energy. The scientific formula for kinetic energy involves both the mass of the moving object and its speed, squared. For example, if someone who weighs 65 pounds (30 kg) rides a bicycle at 10 miles per hour (4.5 m per second), their kinetic energy is about one-sixth of a Calorie (600 joules). In the U.S. system of measurement, a Calorie is one way to express an energy measurement; you may have seen the energy contained in food expressed this way. *Joules* is the unit used in the metric system.

A rocket launch involves burning and releasing the massive amount of energy stored in the rocket's chemical fuel. That energy becomes the energy of the orbiting spacecraft. Even for a small satellite like Vanguard 1, the kinetic energy is impressive: more than 10,000 Calories (43 million joules). By comparison, the International Space Station, now in orbit around Earth, has a mass of more than 1 million pounds (500,000 kg) and its kinetic energy is about 3.5 billion Calories (15 trillion joules).

Another kind of energy is more directly connected to gravity. It is called potential energy. A grapefruit has potential energy when you hold it in your hand because it is in a place where it might fall down. The formula for potential energy involves multiplying the mass of the grapefruit times **g** (which is 32 feet per second squared, or 9.8 meters per second squared) and the distance the grapefruit could fall.

If the grapefruit actually fell, the fall would convert the potential energy to kinetic energy, since the grapefruit would now be moving and, in fact, speed up the longer it fell. Meanwhile, the potential energy decreases as the grapefruit falls because the distance to the ground becomes less and less. Just at the moment when the grapefruit has reached the ground—but before it splits open—its kinetic energy is at its maximum. Upon landing, the potential energy is zero. After the grapefruit hits the ground, the kinetic energy is converted to splattered grapefruit bits.

The launch of a rocket involves not only a lot of kinetic energy, but also quite a lot of potential energy. The Vanguard 1 satellite entered Earth's orbit about 400 miles (650 km) above the ground. Its potential energy there was 2,100 Calories (9 million joules). Once the rocket engine shut down at the end of the launch and the satellite coasted in the orbit, the sum of the potential energy and kinetic energy was fixed. Thanks to an eastward launch of the rocket, the rotation of Earth contributes a little (less than 1%) of the required energy.

Spacecraft Voyages

This is where Kepler's law about ellipses takes over: Vanguard 1's orbit is much more oblong than any planet's orbit in the solar system. In a single orbit, Vanguard 1 climbs up to a height of 2,500 miles (4,000 km) before swooping back down to a height of 400 miles (650 km). On the upward part of its path, Vanguard 1's potential energy increases considerably while the kinetic energy is reduced by that same amount. At its highest point, called the **apogee**, potential energy is at a maximum while kinetic energy is at a minimum, and Vanguard 1 is moving at the slowest speed of its entire orbit. Then when Vanguard 1 swings around, it is quite literally falling, losing potential energy and gaining kinetic energy back again so that its total energy remains the same. Once it gets back to the lowest point, called the **perigee**, the orbit starts over again.

Although orbital speed calculations are extremely complicated, places like NASA's Jet Propulsion Laboratory have specialized in this type of study. During the past 50 years, many spacecraft have been sent on bold missions around the solar system. The Sun—rather than Earth—is the source of gravity for these spacecraft, and the paths they travel run to billions of miles. Spacecraft going to Venus or Mercury, which are the only planets closer to the Sun than Earth, literally have to fall down partway to the Sun under careful control of the people who plan the mission. But if a spacecraft is going to Mars or the outer planets, it must be on an oblong orbit that climbs up against the Sun's gravity. Clever mission design can take advantage of a close pass by a planet to greatly boost a spacecraft's speed.

THE PIONEER MYSTERY

The Pioneer 10 and Pioneer 11 space probes were launched in the 1970s and successfully completed their missions to the outer solar system. Inertia carried them out beyond the planets, and they will continue farther and farther into space. Communication with them was lost a few years ago, but scientists still have a rich amount of data from the probes, including the facts for a persistent puzzle. As the probes traveled away from Earth on their multi-billion mile paths, the Sun's gravity—as predicted—slowed them down considerably.

But something else also made them slow down just a tiny bit more than the astronomers predicted. Think of it like this: if you were coasting along on your bicycle and your brakes slowed you down the same way the mysterious acceleration is slowing down the Pioneers, it would take you 160 years to come to a stop! Despite the incredibly gentle pull, scientists are sure the mysterious observations about the Pioneer probes are not mistakes, because both probes showed the same effect. There have been many suggestions about what may be causing the slow-down, but none have yet been proven.

The New Horizons robot explorer was launched on January 19, 2006. It was given a faster takeoff speed than any other spacecraft before it, and passed the Moon in mere hours. By March of 2007, it had already passed Jupiter. As it passed, it came up on Jupiter from behind and swept into the zone where Jupiter's gravity was stronger than the Sun's gravity. Jupiter's gravity pulled the robot along, increasing the robot's kinetic energy by about 20%. The increase in speed whipped New Horizons forward in its orbit and past Jupiter, where it was again dominated by the Sun's gravity. At this time it was traveling much faster than before, but note that no new energy was created. Rather, a tiny part of Jupiter's own orbital energy was transferred to New Horizons.

New Horizons's mission and destination is now Pluto. Even starting from Jupiter at a speed of 51,000 miles per hour (23,000 meters per second), New Horizons won't arrive at Pluto until July 2015. The closest it will get to the dwarf planet will be a distance of 16,800 miles (27,000 km). Scientists and engineers have calculated the path of the determined little robot so precisely that they already know it will pass by Pluto just 51 minutes after its closest approach. Scientists are able to find this out because the mathematical calculations for gravity are so exact.

Solar System Bombardment

Natural objects in outer space such as comets and asteroids also follow precise paths determined by gravity. There are millions of these objects, of every size, from as big as Texas down to as small as a grapefruit. Many of them pass close enough to Jupiter or one of the other major planets that gravity from those planets as well as gravity from the Sun must be calculated. Throughout millions of years, the orbits of many of these smaller solar system bodies are altered, sometimes repeatedly. Gravity has collected quite a family of asteroids, for example, at points ahead of and behind Jupiter in its orbit around the Sun. These asteroids are called the Trojan asteroids.

In 1994, a comet known as Shoemaker-Levy 9 plowed into Jupiter's atmosphere. Anyone with a small telescope could see the

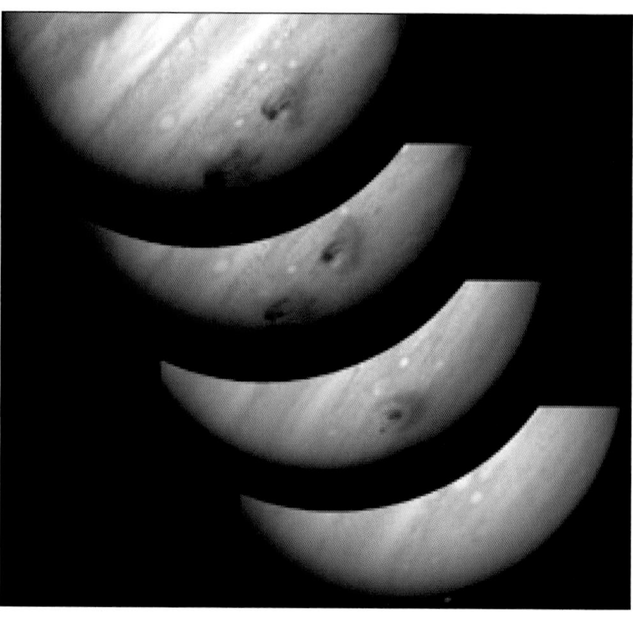

In 1994, comet Shoemaker-Levy 9 collided with Jupiter. The sequence of images (*from top to bottom*), taken by the Hubble Space Telescope, was photographed five minutes, two hours, and then several days after the collision.

THE MONSTER AT THE HEART OF THE GALAXY

Gravity does much more than determine the tides and move spaceships. It determines the shape of entire planets. Notice when you look at a drawing of the solar system that all the planets are round. This is simply because the bulk of a planet is drawn toward the planet's center as much as possible. Even the shape of the whole galaxy is influenced by gravity.

Gravity also makes stars burn as brightly as they do. Gravity squeezes the hydrogen gas in the core of a star so tightly that the gas turns to helium. The squeezing of the hydrogen is called nuclear fusion, and it releases so much energy that the entire star shines brightly.

But perhaps the most exciting and mysterious effect that gravity has on space is the formation of black holes. A black hole is an object so incredibly dense (tightly packed) that its gravity is strong enough to prevent everything—even light—from escaping. All the matter in six Earths would have to be squeezed together in order to make a black hole the size of a grapefruit.

In the year 2000, astronomers measured X-rays coming from the center of the Milky Way galaxy and found evidence that there is a gigantic black hole there. This monster black hole is called Sagittarius A* (say "A-star" if you read it out loud), and it contains the mass of almost 4 million stars the size of the Sun. Fortunately for Earth, the center of the galaxy is 160 million billion miles (240 million billion km) away.

awesome power of gravity on display. Jupiter's gravitational pull first tore Shoemaker-Levy 9 into about two dozen chunks. Each of the chunks made an impressive splash in the uppermost cloud layers of the giant planet. Comets and asteroids have crashed into all the planets and moons of the solar system over time, creating such features as the cratered surface of the Moon.

In fact, collisions on Earth are one of the major challenges for life on this planet. About 65 million years ago, Earth's gravity brought down a chunk of rock or ice in space that was about 10 miles (16 km) wide. It hit the coast of Mexico and the explosion is believed to have caused massive changes in Earth's environment. Many scientists believe that those changes killed off a large percentage of the dinosaur population of that time. Collisions like this one are rare on Earth, but smaller objects frequently enter the atmosphere. These smaller objects—meteors—burn up in Earth's atmosphere without causing such a catastrophe. They can be seen on most clear, dark nights. Some are large enough to light up the sky for several seconds, but most appear as thin streaks of light.

CHAPTER FIVE

Einstein's Universe

The planet Mercury, nearest to the Sun, orbits the inner solar system in 88 Earth days. That's the quickest complete orbit of any planet. Mercury's path brings it within 28,600,000 miles (46,000,000 km) of the Sun—its closest approach—out to a maximum distance of 43,500,000 miles (70,000,000 km). This is the largest climb and descent of any major planet in the Sun's gravity. Mercury is also locked in a peculiar spinning dance with the Sun. Mercury spins around slowly—59 days go by on Earth in the time it takes Mercury to spin around once. Since 59 × 3 and 88 × 2 both equal about 177, two Mercury years pass in almost exactly three Mercury days. The folks on Mercury would have two New Year's celebrations in just three Mercury days.

Around the same time that Le Verrier studied the orbit mystery of the planet Uranus, astronomers noticed that each time Mercury swung around the Sun, the moment of its closest approach happened just a little bit later than the previous time. It wasn't much: just about a minute and a half. After 88 Earth days, a minute and a half may not seem like a lot. But of course, that adds up over many orbits. Before the nineteenth century, scientists wouldn't have worried about the discrepancy. After scientists were able to make such incredibly precise astronomical measurements, however, they wanted to understand why this happened. Astronomers came up with a couple of reasons why Mercury's closest approach didn't always happen at exactly the same time in its orbit.

Astronomers made great progress in solving this mystery, but in the end, there was still about half a second of time difference in each orbit that could not be explained. Just as Kepler based his new theory of Mars on a very small difference between a measured angle and a predicted angle, astronomers were determined to figure out what was behind the differences in Mercury's orbit from year to year.

The Theory of Relativity

Albert Einstein came up with an improvement to Newton's laws of motion and gravity. In 1905, Einstein began introducing new formulas that became known all together as the theory of relativity. The first part of the theory, called the theory of special relativity, is about the speed of light. It explains what happens when objects move extremely fast. The second part of the theory of relativity is on general relativity. In general relativity, Einstein outlined something very important about the actual shape of space: when straight lines are close to very massive or heavy objects, gravity makes those lines curve slightly. The effect is hardly noticeable, even for something as large as planet Earth. But closer to the Sun, where the Sun's gravity is stronger, there is enough of a curve in space to pull an object along just a little bit farther than it would otherwise go. Einstein calculated the effect of curved space on the differences observed in the planet Mercury's orbit, and it came out remarkably close to the mysterious missing half-second. Astronomers were very impressed by this aspect of the new theory.

An even more impressive demonstration of the general theory of relativity came in 1919. Since light from a distant star always follows a straight line, then the position of a distant star, as it is seen in the sky, should be a little bit off if the light must curve

GRAVITY PROBE B

Gravity Probe B might turn out to be the most important space satellite ever launched for science. Einstein had overlooked the idea of testing general relativity with very stable gyroscopes. A gyroscope is a small disk or sphere that doesn't fall down because it spins very fast. Gyroscopes are much smaller and spin much more quickly than planets and stars, and they show the long-term influence of gravity much sooner. The equations for general relativity predict that there would be two extremely slight effects of gravity on a gyroscope. One effect occurs because a gyroscope should wobble just a bit when a planet is nearby. The second effect would make the gyroscopes built into Gravity Probe B turn around one extra rotation every 31,000,000 years. It seems incredible, but scientists expect to be able to measure this extra turning movement in just a few years of operation.

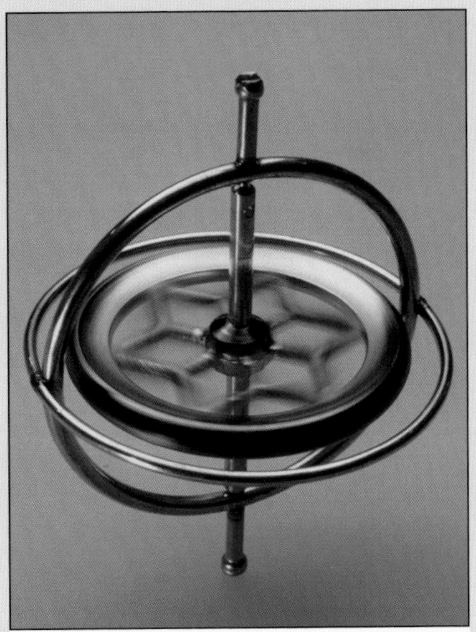

A gyroscope consists of a spinning wheel mounted on an axle so that its axis can turn freely in certain directions. It is capable of maintaining the same absolute direction despite movements of the axle or surrounding elements.

The space probe has four sphere-shaped gyroscopes made of quartz. They are supported inside the spaceship by an electric system. In April 2004, Gravity Probe B was launched to an orbit 400 miles (640 kilometers) high, and was sent traveling over Earth's north and south poles. Measurements of the gyroscopes were made in 2005 and 2006. When the results are announced, scientists might have the best proof yet for Einstein's work.

slightly around a huge mass like the Sun. No one had ever noticed the positions of stars so close to the Sun before, and for good reason: when the Sun is in the sky, it's daytime, and other stars can't be seen—except, that is, during a total eclipse of the Sun. For this reason, scientists measured the positions of stars close by the Sun during an eclipse in 1919.

Indeed, the observations supported Einstein's ideas. Better measurements were made when other eclipses occurred, such as in 1922. New and improved measuring techniques were always being developed, and so the measurements became more precise as time passed. Then, in the early 1990s, the Hipparcos space satellite made the most accurate measurements yet of star positions as the Sun passed in front of the stars. The results confirmed yet again Einstein's general theory of relativity.

There have also been other efforts to test Einstein's general theory. Every test so far has confirmed that the theory is a good way to explain the way objects function in the real world. One very practical effect involves the Global Positioning System (GPS)

Global Positioning System (GPS) satellites are used for navigational purposes. The GPS calculates the curving of radio signals from the satellites to determine various positions on Earth. Some cars now have GPS mapping abilities so drivers can easily get directions.

satellites. With a GPS receiver, people can tell their precise location on Earth's surface. The computer programming for the GPS includes calculations for the curving of radio signals from the satellites. If general relativity were not included in the computer programming, a GPS receiver would not be so useful.

Perhaps what is most exciting about general relativity is that it offers the first basic explanation for why gravity exists at all. Neither Newton nor any other scientist before Einstein had ever come up with a reasonable suggestion. How does matter—the actual stuff anything is made of—somehow manage to reach across empty space and pull something? By tying gravity to the shape of space, Einstein took some of the mystery out of it. Since it seems reasonable to think of the motion of an object as following a straight line all the time, the fact that gravity alters the shape of a straight line helps explain the actual path of an object in space.

Gravity's Lens

In recent years, astronomers have been able to observe the curve of space by looking through powerful telescopes at extremely distant galaxies and **quasars**. Even though galaxies and quasars are enormous objects, some of them appear tiny because they are so incredibly far away. Astronomers often use light years to express the size of galaxies and the distance to them. A **light year** is actually a measure of distance, not time. One light year is the distance light travels in one Earth year—365.25 days. This distance works out to be almost 6 trillion miles (9 trillion km). A typical galaxy like the Milky Way is about 100,000 light years across. Galaxies are usually separated from each other by many millions of light years of empty space.

In a few cases, the light from one of the most distant galaxies must pass nearby another galaxy that happens to lie between it and Earth. For example, Abell 2218 is a cluster of galaxies about 3 billion light years from Earth. In the same direction as Abell 2218 are other galaxies that are three or four times farther away.

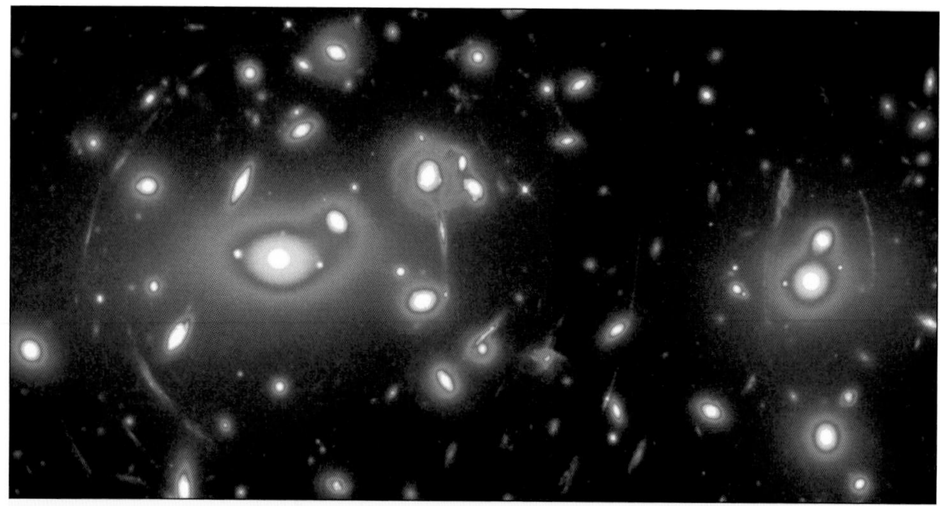

Galaxy cluster Abell 2218 is approximately 3 billion light years away from Earth, and it is so large that light rays from galaxies in the background pass through it and are deflected and magnified by the cluster's gravity. Abell 2218 serves as a gravitational lens that gives an image of even farther galaxies.

The gravity of Abell 2218 bends the light from the more distant galaxies so that our view of them is distorted in complicated ways. Modern computer programs can calculate the distortion so precisely that scientists are able to get an accurate picture of how the matter is spread out in the cluster in between.

Is Gravity Really Universal?

With the impressive successes in cracking the mysteries of the universe, you might think that scientists are completely in agreement about the rules of gravity. But the field of science encourages a healthy skepticism. There will always be a hint of doubt that perhaps the measurements could be refined or improved, or that perhaps the formula itself is not quite perfect. Although researchers do not take all suggestions seriously, there are some ideas that are worth examining here.

One is the possibility that gravity changes over time. Perhaps the strength of gravity varies, so that it slowly gets stronger and then weaker again. Or could it be that gravity was stronger in the past and will be weaker in the future? Paul Dirac, a physicist who won the Nobel Prize in 1933, made this suggestion. But it's enormously difficult to make such sensitive measurements. In 1998, a team of astronomers checked out small vibrations in the Sun that are affected by gravity the same way a bouncing ball is. Data came from six separate telescopes, and the astronomers concluded that no major change in the strength of gravity has taken place during the past few billion years. If there were a change in gravity, it would have to have been extraordinarily tiny.

The 1919 Solar Eclipse Expeditions

Einstein's discoveries made headlines around the world. The *London Times* called the theory of relativity a "Revolution in Science. New Theory of the Universe." But Einstein did not become the most famous scientist in the world overnight. From 1911 until 1915, he worked on a formula for how much a ray of light would be deflected as it passed by a huge object like the Sun. It wasn't

A total solar eclipse is when the Sun is completely covered by the Moon. The 1919 solar eclipse (*left*), which was photographed and studied in an expedition led by physicist Sir Arthur Eddington, proved Albert Einstein's theory of relativity. Scientists observed the position of the stars during the eclipse and then compared their calculations to the position of stars during a regular night.

until an expedition from England set out to test his theories that Einstein became famous outside of the scientific community.

Astronomers in England heard about Einstein's calculations. They put together an expedition to observe starlight during the total solar eclipse on May 29, 1919, and to compare the positions of the stars during the eclipse to the positions of the same stars during regular nighttime. This was before the days of jet planes; it was also during World War I, which tore apart much of Europe, including England. This meant that a lot of prior planning had to be done for the expedition.

Two teams left England in February 1919 so they would have time to set up their instruments. One team went to the coast of Africa, and the other went to Brazil. It wasn't easy for either of them. One team had cloudy skies, and the other had a problem with the focus of its main telescope. The expeditions only collected a few useful pictures, which took months more to analyze. The results were finally presented at a scientific meeting in London at the beginning of November 1919.

CHAPTER SIX

Dark Matter

Gravity is actually very weak when compared with other forces such as electricity. So why is gravity important at all? The reason is that gravity is the only force that works across wide spaces and keeps piling up between large objects. The gravity force holding the Moon in orbit around Earth is 2 million trillion trillion times stronger than the gravity force between two small objects, such as books, held on either side of you. Compare this to what the electric force is between Earth and the Moon: zero. But there is no such thing as neutral gravity, because gravity acts upon all objects, no matter how small. On the cosmic scale, gravity is king.

Zwicky's Galaxies

Using Kepler's laws for orbits and Newton's equations for gravity, scientists can understand how matter fits together right out to the deepest regions of outer space. In the 1930s, astronomer Fritz Zwicky measured the motions of individual galaxies near the edge of a large galaxy cluster more than 300 million light years from Earth. Zwicky was surprised by the results: according to his calculations, the total amount of matter in the cluster was more than 400 times more than the material visible in photographs. Could there really be some kind of matter that couldn't be seen, even in such colossal quantities? For many years, Zwicky's discovery was filed away as an unexplained puzzle—no more than a curiosity.

The motions of stars and star clusters in the Milky Way galaxy were measured with radio telescopes in the 1950s. Astronomers compared these motions and expected that they would learn about how material was spread out in the inner regions of the galaxy. After all, for moving things like spacecraft, moons, and planets, the source of gravity is the Sun or a major planet at the center of their orbits. This means the source of gravity is a single concentrated object. But a galaxy is spread out over a vast area of space, and for a star or cluster moving around a whole galaxy, the source of gravity is not concentrated in one spot. For the main part of the galaxy, scientists found that Kepler's laws and Newton's equations explained the motion rather well.

Then in the 1970s, another astronomer, Vera Rubin, looked at many other galaxies and noticed a peculiar fact about the way they rotate. Her observations showed that stars and star clusters in the outer regions of a galaxy do not wheel around in the expected way.

Rubin noticed that motion farther away from the center of a galaxy followed a somewhat different equation from Kepler's Laws. After making the appropriate calculations, Rubin figured out that there was a lot more matter out beyond the visible part of a spiral-shaped galaxy. For some reason, this matter could not be seen.

In science, invisible things are more difficult to study and so don't fit well into theories. Rubin's research reminded experts of the invisible matter Zwicky predicted, and at first, other astronomers were skeptical about these ideas. Soon, though,

WAVES OF GRAVITY

Light, electricity, and other forms of energy travel in waves. The general theory of relativity predicts that there should also be waves of gravity. Gravity waves occur whenever anything moves, turns, or collides with something else. The theory of general relativity predicted that a ripple of gravity would spread out at the speed of light, getting weaker and weaker the farther it spread. For a small object such as a book, or even an object many times larger, the disturbance in gravity would be unbelievably tiny. But when something of astronomical size—such as a star or a black hole—shakes, bumps, or explodes, the gravity waves are much stronger.

Detecting gravity waves has proven to be an enormous challenge. Very technical equipment and extraordinarily exact measurements are needed. The Laser Interferometer Gravity Wave Observatory, or LIGO, is one project designed to detect gravity waves. LIGO uses laser beams inside vacuum tubes 2.5 miles (4 km) long. If an extremely large gravity wave passes by, the laser beam would detect the movement. Since 2002, scientists at the two LIGO facilities have been watching closely, but they have not succeeded in capturing a gravity wave yet. An even more precise project for LIGO has been proposed for future studies.

A team of computer-savvy relativity experts in Germany prepared this simulated view of gravity waves from two colliding black holes. The different colors show ripples of gravity.

The Hubble Space Telescope, which was launched in April 1990, took this picture of two galaxies, NGC2207 (left) and IC2163, swinging past each other. Gravity creates this 500-million-year cosmic dance.

many other galaxies were studied, and new evidence came up that supported Rubin's conclusion.

Astronomers came to accept that vast amounts of unseen material are located in the outer regions of galaxies and between galaxies grouped together in clusters. Whatever this puzzling stuff is, astronomers started calling it **dark matter**. The challenge is to learn something about it even though it is invisible. Not much has been learned so far in the twenty-first century. So far, the most that astronomers know about dark matter is how much of it there is overall and where most of it is located. As hinted by Zwicky's and Rubin's research, there is about six times more dark matter than ordinary matter in the universe.

Where to Look for Dark Matter

When the Hubble Space Telescope (HST) was launched in 1990, dark matter was still controversial among scientists. Although dark matter can't be seen directly, it reveals itself because of its gravity. Zwicky and Rubin studied the influence of dark matter's gravity on moving objects. Another technique that astronomers used in the 1990s and early in the twenty-first century was to measure how the gravity from dark matter changes. Sophisticated computer software can tell just by looking at the twisted images of background galaxies how much dark matter is in the galaxy or cluster of galaxies in front of it.

In 2007, a team of 70 Hubble Space Telescope researchers announced the results of a major project, called COSMOS, which would map the presence of dark matter over many millions of light years. The telescope first took 575 separate but overlapping photographs. Individual galaxies in the same zone of space were also measured in greater detail by three large telescopes on mountaintops in Hawaii and Chile. The combined data confirmed that dark matter stretches through space like cobwebs.

STRING THEORY

The ultimate goal of modern science is to explain how the world works with the fewest possible rules—maybe even just one. Some scientists call this goal the theory of everything. So far, experts have managed to roll up light, magnetism, electricity, and all the observations about what happens inside the atomic nucleus into a theory known as the standard model. But they have not been able to make gravity fit with the standard model.

One fascinating idea that does include gravity is string theory. In string theory (or M-Theory, as it is sometimes called), all atoms, molecules, beams of light, and every object in the universe are really built out of unbelievably tiny loops of vibrating string. In fact, the size of these strings is so small that just breaking them out of ordinary particles would take more energy than any scientific experiment yet dreamed of. What the string itself is made of isn't nearly so important as how it vibrates. At this point in the twenty-first century, no direct proof for string theory has been found, but some experts think that large-scale gravity might turn out to be caused by the shape of these vibrating strings.

Where the webs of dark matter cross, clumps are formed. Galaxies are sprinkled through space, but always along the strands of dark matter. Throughout billions of years, gravity from the clumps of dark matter draws the galaxies into clusters. In between the strands of dark matter are great empty spaces where

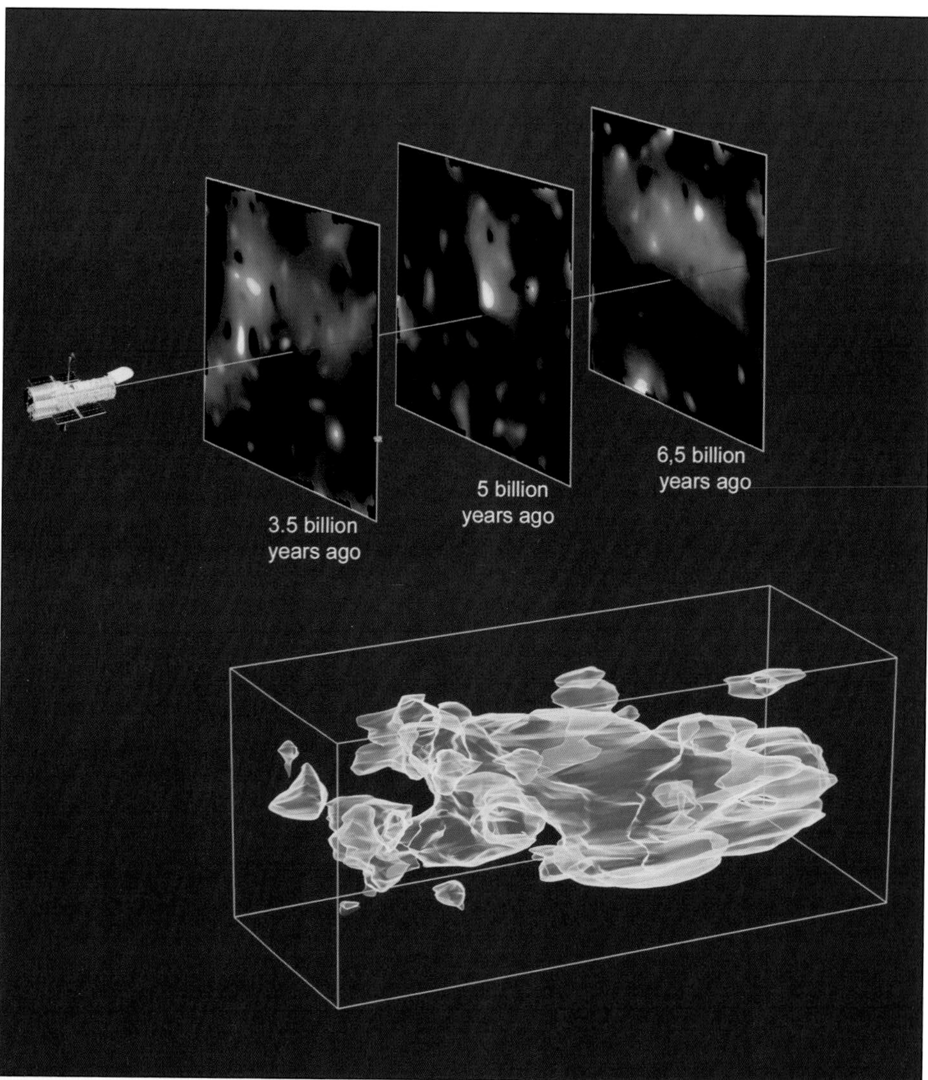

This 3-dimensional view of where invisible dark matter has been for more than hundreds of millions of light years was put together from 1,000 hours of Hubble Space Telescope photography, as well as observations by some of the largest telescopes on Earth.

it seems that there is almost no dark matter to be found. Galaxies are rare there. On the largest possible scale, it appears the universe resembles a sponge with gaps of nothingness in between the strands of dark matter and galaxies.

The actual nature of dark matter is still entirely mysterious. One suggestion has been that dark matter is made of planet-sized chunks of ordinary matter that are so cold they do not give off any light at all. This theory has been tested, and no such support for it has yet been found. Meanwhile, dark matter has never been observed in any laboratory on Earth. Two experiments, one at Gran Sasso, Italy, and the other in a mine in Minnesota, have searched for the presence of dark matter. These experiments are based on the idea that dark matter might be made of extremely microscopic particles. Still, no one knows for sure, so perhaps a scientist in the twenty-first century will eventually discover the nature of dark matter.

The Origin and Fate of the Universe

Scientists in general accept the idea that the universe began at a single point with an explosion known as the **big bang**. All the matter and energy—including the dark matter—and all the patterns in space in every direction were all determined more or less by the details of the big bang. Extremely tiny ripples in the explosion were the starting points for the strands of dark matter that stretch everywhere.

The leftover heat from the big bang can still be seen today. An Earth-orbiting satellite took a detailed picture of these leftovers in 2003. The picture showed splotches where the big bang was just a tiny bit hotter or cooler than average. Calculations based on this data matched what experts had figured the pattern of splotches would look like, and this explained how the strands of dark matter and galaxies got their start.

Scientists don't know much about gravity's role in the very early universe. The origin of other forces, such as the electric force and the nuclear forces, can be calculated backward almost

THE PERIMETER INSTITUTE

A scientific institute gives researchers the opportunity to focus on their work. That's what an institute is all about: brilliant scientists working together so they can share ideas and help each other when they get stumped. In 1999, a new center for the study of basic questions in astronomy and physics, such as string theory, was established in Waterloo, Canada. Called the Perimeter Institute, it is supported both by donations from businesses and the Canadian government.

Sometimes the hardest part of forming a strong scientific institute is to create a feeling of independence for the researchers, so they don't get distracted from their studies. Perhaps what is most important about a place like the Perimeter Institute is that its work inspires everyone to think about the universe in a sensible way. The Perimeter Institute reaches out with public lectures, workshops for teachers and young students, videos that are available on the Internet, and even a program of orchestra concerts. Even the design of their new building is intended to inspire cleverness and attract new scientific minds.

to the moment of the big bang itself. But in the first tiny fractions of the universe's first few seconds, everything was packed in so incredibly tightly that Einstein's equations for gravity give unclear results.

A new formula is needed to explain what gravity would be like under those astounding conditions. Such a new formula would be called quantum gravity. String theory is one of the ideas that experts are studying for quantum gravity. If a scientist were to come up with a new formula that could be tested in an experiment, or at least fit in with the other ideas about the big bang, it would be a huge sensation.

What will happen in the future? Ever since the big bang, space itself has been expanding. The dark matter and all the galaxies have spread out to where they are today, and they will continue to spread out. For decades, astronomers debated whether gravity would pull the universe back together once all the other forces weakened and cancelled each other. Then in 1997, some shocking news was revealed: the universe can never stop expanding because the expansion is forever speeding up. Every place in the universe will eventually be completely isolated and neither light nor any other form of energy will cross the empty gulf of space. So in the end, trillions and trillions of years from now, not even gravity will have any meaning. Beyond that, science cannot yet speculate.

Glossary

acceleration – any change in speed, or even a change in the direction of motion. The word comes from the Latin words that mean "to speed up."

apogee – the farthest point that a satellite reaches in its orbit around Earth

big bang – the theory that an explosion started the universe about 13.7 billion years ago

black hole – an object so incredibly dense that gravity on its surface is strong enough to prevent everything, even light, from escaping

dark matter – invisible stuff concentrated in the outer regions of a galaxy and in between galaxies. Although its nature is unknown, astronomers calculate that there is about six times as much dark matter as regular matter in the whole universe.

eclipse – an event that occurs when a body in space, such as a planet, lines up with two others, such as a moon and the Sun

ellipse – a geometric shape in which every point along its outline is the same total distance from two fixed points near its center. An ellipse looks like a stretched-out circle.

energy – the ability to make things happen. Any situation in which a force could be made to push an object from one spot to another spot involves energy somehow.

experiment – a situation or event specially arranged to test whether something works or whether a suggested explanation makes sense

focus – either of the two fixed points near the center of an ellipse, used to measure the total distance out to any point on the ellipse

force – a push or a pull

gravity – a force that exists between any two objects in the universe, as calculated by Isaac Newton's formula for gravity. The word *gravity* also refers to the theories and scientific laws that have been developed to explain the force of gravity.

inertia – the property that causes an object to keep doing what it's already doing

kinetic energy – the energy a moving object has just because it is moving

light year – the distance light travels across the vacuum of space in 365.25 days at a speed of 670,616,629.384 miles per hour (299,792,458 meters per second). One light year is about 5,879,000,000,000 miles (9,460,730,472,580,800 meters).

orbit – the path of any natural or artificial object in space as it travels around a larger object under the influence of gravity

perigee – the point in a satellite's orbit around Earth when the satellite and Earth are closest together

period – the time required for a body to come back to the same point in its orbit

quasar – the most distant objects known in the universe. A quasar is the core of an enormous galaxy, and it gives off as much light and radiation as the rest of the entire galaxy around it. This likely happens because there is a black hole in the core that has already absorbed millions of stars the size of the Sun.

square – in arithmetic, to "square" a number means to multiply a number by itself. For instance, the square of 3 is 9 because $3 \times 3 = 9$. In a formula, this amounts to multiplying or dividing by a number twice.

theory – a likely explanation for something that happens in real life

weight – the force of gravity on any object. Usually this refers to gravity at the surface of Earth.

Bibliography

"Anomalous Precessions," Reflections on Relativity. Available online. URL: www.mathpages.com/rr/s6-02/6-02.htm.

Asimov, Isaac. *Understanding Physics: Motion, Sound, and Heat.* New York: Walker and Company, 1966.

Bartusiak, Marcia. *Through a Universe Darkly: A Cosmic Tale of Ancient Ethers, Dark Matter, and the Fate of the Universe.* New York: HarperCollins, 1993.

"Basics of Space Flight: Participant's Guide," NASA Jet Propulsion Laboratory. Available online. URL: http://www2.jpl.nasa.gov/basics/guide.html.

"Basics of Space Flight: Section II," NASA Jet Propulsion Laboratory. Available online. URL: http://www2.jpl.nasa.gov/basics/bsf9-1.html.

Bergmann, Peter G. *The Riddle of Gravitation.* New York: Charles Scribner's Sons, 1987.

Britt, Robert Roy. "The Problem with Gravity: New Mission Would Probe Strange Puzzle," Space.com. Available online.
URL: www.space.com/scienceastronomy/mystery_monday_041018.html.

Butlin, Chris. "Chris Butlin's Yorkshire Snippets Henry Cavendish and 'G,'" Yorkshire Physics News. Available online.
URL: www.physics.leeds.ac.uk/physics/newsletters/january99/jan99.htm#jan99-5.

Ciufolini, Ignazio, and John Archibald Wheeler. *Gravitation and Inertia.* Princeton, N.J.: Princeton University Press, 1995.

Drake, Stillman. *History of Free Fall.* Toronto: Wall & Thompson, 1989.

Feynman, Richard. *The Character of Physical Law.* Cambridge, Mass.: M.I.T. Press, 1965.

Fisher, Leonard Everett. *Galileo.* New York: Macmillan, 1992.

Fowler, Michael. "Galileo's Acceleration Experiment," University of Virginia Physics Department. Available online.
URL: http://galileoandeinstein.physics.virginia.edu/lectures/gal_accn96.htm.

"Great Minds—Great Thinkers: Isaac Newton," EDinformatics. Available online. URL: www.edinformatics.com/great_thinkers/newton.htm.

Greene, Brian. *The Elegant Universe: Superstrings, Hidden Dimensions, and the Quest for the Ultimate Theory.* New York: W. W. Norton & Company, 1999.

Gribbin, John, and Mary Gribbin. *Time & Space.* Toronto: Stoddart, 1994.

Haas, Jason. "Albert Einstein for Kids," Wesleyan University. Available online. URL: www.wesleyan.edu/synthesis/culture-cubed/haas/maintemp.htm.

Hawking, Stephen. *A Brief History of Time.* New York: Bantam, 1988.

Hawking, Stephen. *The Universe in a Nutshell.* New York: Bantam, 2001.

Ipsen, D.C. *Isaac Newton, Reluctant Genius.* Hillside, N.J.: Enslow, 1985.

"Kidinnu, the Chaldaeans, and Babylonian Astronomy," Livius. Available online. URL: www.livius.org/k/kidinnu/kidinnu.htm.

Kirshner, Robert P. *The Extravagant Universe: Exploding Stars, Dark Energy, and the Accelerating Cosmos.* Princeton, N.J.: Princeton University Press, 2004.

Krauss, Lawrence M. *Quintessence: The Mystery of the Missing Mass*. New York: Basic Books, 2001.

Laser Interferometer Gravitational-Wave Observatory. Available online. URL: www.ligo.caltech.edu/.

MacLachlan, James. *Galileo Galilei: First Physicist*. Oxford, U.K.: Oxford University Press, 1997.

Maldacena, Juan. "The Illusion of Gravity." *Scientific American* (November 2005): 57.

McTavish, Douglas. *Isaac Newton*. East Sussex, U.K.: Wayland, 1990.

Milgrom, Harry. *First Experiments with Gravity*. New York: E.P. Dutton, 1966.

"Orbital Velocity and Period Calculator," Exploration. Available online. URL: http://liftoff.msfc.nasa.gov/academy/rocket_sci/orbmech/vel_calc.html.

Perimeter Institute for Theoretical Physics. Available online. URL: www.perimeterinstitute.ca.

Plant, David. "Tycho Brahe: A King Amongst Astronomers," Skyscript. Available online. URL: www.skyscript.co.uk/brahe.html.

Recording of Sputnik 1 radio transmission. Available online. URL: www.mentallandscape.com/V_Sputnik.mp3.

Reisch, George. "Think Pieces: Audio Legends," Stereophile. Available online. URL: http://stereophile.com/thinkpieces/1197audio/.

Sartori, Leo. *Understanding Relativity: A Simplified Approach to Einstein's Theory*. Berkeley: University of California Press, 1996.

Severance, John B. *Einstein: Visionary Scientist*. New York: Clarion Books, 1999.

Sheldrake, Rupert. "The Variability of Fundamental Constants," Sheldrake online. Available online. URL: www.sheldrake.org/experiments/constants/.

"Shoot a Cannonball into Orbit!" NASA Space Place. Available online. URL: http://spaceplace.jpl.nasa.gov/en/kids/orbits1.shtml.

Simon, Sheridan, *Unlocking the Universe: A Biography of Stephen Hawking*. Minneapolis, Minn.: Dillon Press, 1991.

Skurzynski, Gloria. *Zero Gravity*. New York: Bradbury Press, 1994.

Snyder, Dave. "Gravity, Part 2: Newton, Hooke, Halley and the Three Body Problem," University Lowbrow Astronomers. Available online. URL: http://www.umich.edu/~lowbrows/reflections/2006/dsnyder.17.html.

Wheeler, John Archibald, and E.F. Taylor. *Spacetime Physics*. San Francisco: W.H. Freeman, 1966.

Further Exploration

BOOKS

Krull, Kathleen. *Isaac Newton.* New York: Viking, 2006.

Lauw, Darlene. *Motion.* New York: Crabtree Publishing, 2002.

Nardo, Don. *Black Holes.* Farmington Hills, Mich.: Lucent Books, 2004.

Oxlade, Chris. *Gravity.* Chicago: Heinemann Library, 2007.

Panchyk, Richard. *Galileo for Kids: His Life and Ideas.* Chicago: Chicago Review Press, 2005.

Trumbauer, Lisa. *What is Gravity?* New York: Children's Press, 2004.

WEB SITES

History of gravity

http://galileoandeinstein.physics.virginia.edu/lectures/gal_accn96.htm
A descriptive summary of how Galileo came up with some of the key ideas about motion and gravity.

Orbit speed calculator

http://liftoff.msfc.nasa.gov/academy/rocket_sci/orbmech/vel_calc.html
Enter a height above the ground and the site will describe the orbit for you.

Theory of Relativity

http://whyfiles.org/052einstein/frame_drag4.html
An explanation of Einstein's theory of relativity.

Index

Page numbers for illustrations are in *italic*.

Abell 2218 galaxy, 44–45, *45*
acceleration, 10
Almagest, The (Ptolemy), 15–16, *17*
apogee, 36
apple, Newton's, 26
Aristarchus of Samos, 18
Aristotle, 8
asteroids, 39–40

Babylonian astronomy, 15
big bang, 55
black holes, 39, *51*, 51
Brahe, Tycho, 19, 20

Cavendish, Henry, 28
comet collisions, 38–40
comet orbits, 30
Copernicus, Nicolaus, 19
COSMOS, 53

dark matter, 49–55, *54*
days of week, 18

Earth, comet and asteroid collisions with, 39–40
eclipses
  lunar, 15, *16*
  solar, 44, *47*, 47–48
Einstein, Albert, 42–45, 47–48
ellipse, 19, 22, *22*
energy
  defined, 34
  kinetic energy, 34–35
  potential energy, 35–36
experiments, 7, 8–9

focus of ellipse, 19, 22
force, defined, 27

g (acceleration of gravity), 29, 35
galaxies, 44–45, 45, 49–52, 52. *See also* Milky Way
Galileo Galilei, 10–14, *12*
general theory of relativity, 42–45
Global Positioning System (GPS), *44*, 44–45
gravitational constant, 27–29
gravity, law of, 8
Gravity Probe B, 43
gravity waves, 51, *51*
Greek science, 8
gyroscopes, 43, *43*

Halley, Edmund, *30*
Halley's comet, 30
heliocentric system, 18–19
Hipparcos space satellite, 44
Hubble Space Telescope (HST), *52*, 52–53, *54*

inertia, 14, 24
International Space Station, 35
International System of measurement, 9

joules, 35
Jupiter, *38*, 38–39

Kepler, Johannes, 19, 21–23, 26
Kepler's laws, 19, 21–23, *22*
kinetic energy, 34–35

Laser Interferometer Gravity Wave Observatory (LIGO), 51
Le Verrier, Urbain Jean Joseph, 34
light years, 44
LIGO (Laser Interferometer Gravity Wave Observatory), 51
lunar eclipses, 15, *16*

mass, 27, 31
measurement units, 9
measurements, scientific, 8–9
Mercury, 41–42
meteors, 40
metric system of measurement, 9
Milky Way, 39, 44, 49–50
moon
  eclipses of, 15, *16*
  influence on tides, 29
  Newton's calculation of orbit of, 26
  in Ptolemy's system, 16
motion, laws of, 24–26
M-Theory, 53

Neptune, 34, *34*
New Horizons robot explorer, 37–38
Newton, Sir Isaac, 24–28, *25*, 29, 30, 34
Newton's apple, 26
1919 solar eclipse expedition, 47–48
numbers, use in science, 8–9

observatories, Brahe's, 20, *20*
orbit
of comets, 30
defined, 26
of moon, 26
of planets, 19, 21–23, *22*. *See also* planetary motion
orbital speed calculations, 36–38

perigee, 36
Perimeter Institute, 56
period, 21
Philosophiae Naturalis Principia Mathematica (Newton), *25*
Pioneer space probes, 37
Pisa, Italy, 13
planetary motion
days of the week and, 18
heliocentric theory of, 18–19
Kepler's laws of, 19, 21–23, *22*
Ptolemy's theory of, 15–18
planets. *See also* Earth; Jupiter; Mercury; Neptune; Uranus
orbits of, 19–23, *22*
origin of word, 16
period of, 21
shape of, 39
speed of, 21
potential energy, 35–36
Ptolemy, Claudius, 15–18, *17*

quantum gravity, 56
quasars, 44

ramp experiments of Galileo, 10–14, *12*
relativity, theory of, 42–45, 47–48
rocket launches, 32–33, *33*, 35–36
Rubin, Vera, 50, 52, 53

Sagittarius A*, 39
scientific experiments, 7, 8–9
scientific laws, 8
scientific theories, testing of, 7–8
Shoemaker-Levy 9 comet, *38*, 38–39
solar eclipses, 44, *47*, 47–48
solar system bombardment, 38–40
space race, 32
spacecraft voyages, 36–38
special relativity, theory of, 42
Sputnik 1, 32
square, 22, 27
stars
early explanations of movement of, 15–19
nuclear fusion in, 39
Stjerneborg observatory, 20, *20*
string theory, 53, 56
sun. *See also* solar system
eclipses of, 44, *47*, 47–48
in heliocentric system, 18
in Kepler's system, 19, 21, *22*
in Ptolemy's system, 16

theories, testing of, 7–8
theory of relativity, 42–45, 47–48
thrown objects, motion of, 24–26
tides, 29
time measurements by Galileo, 12
torsion balance, *28*, 28–29
Tower of Pisa, 13, *13*

units of measurement, 9
universal gravitation, law of, 26–28, 46–47
universe
heliocentric theory of, 18–19
Kepler's laws and, 19, 21–23, *22*
origin and fate of, 55–57
Ptolemy's theory of planetary and stellar movement, 15–18
Uraniborg observatory, 20
Uranus, 34

Vanguard 1, 32, 35–36
variations in gravity, 46–47

waves of gravity, 51, *51*
week, days of, 18
weight, 31

Zwicky, Fritz, 49–50, 52, 53

About the Author

Peter Jedicke teaches mathematics and science at Fanshawe College in London, Canada. Jedicke studied physics and philosophy and is an active amateur astronomer, involved both locally and nationally in the Royal Astronomical Society of Canada. He has written articles for *Astronomy* and *Sky & Telescope* magazines. His other books include *Cosmology: Exploring the Universe*, *SETI: The Search for Alien Intelligence*, and *Scientific American's The Big Idea*.

Picture Credits

PAGE: 3: Gulfimages/Getty Images
11: Erich Schrempp/Photo Researchers Inc.
12: Scala/Art Resource NY
13: © Fred de Noyelle/Godong/Corbis
16: John Chumack/Photo Researchers Inc.
17: Erich Lessing/Art Resource NY
20: © SSPL/The Image Works
21: John Chumack/Photo Researchers Inc.
22: © Infobase Publishing
25: Art Resource NY
28: © SSPL/The Image Works
30: © Bettmann/Corbis
33: NASA
34: © NASA/Roger Ressmeyer/Corbis
38: Space Telescope Science Institute/NASA/Photo Researchers Inc.
43: E.R. Degginger/Photo Researchers Inc.
44: © Martyn Goddard/Corbis
46: W. Couch & R. Ellis/NASA/Photo Researchers Inc.
47: © Science Museum/SSPL/The Image Works
51: Relativity Group/FSU Jena
52: SPL/Photo Researchers Inc.
54: NASA/ESA/R. Massey (California Institute of Technology)

COVER (*LEFT TO RIGHT*):

Italy's Tower of Pisa is famous for its lean, thanks to gravity. (© Philip Lange)

The moon affects the tides. (© IKO)

A composite image shows NASA's Gravity Prove B satellite above Earth. (© NASA/Photo Researchers)